VERY EASY PIANO TUNES

Anthony Marks

Edited by Jenny Tyler
Designed by Doriana Berkovic

Illustrated by Simone Abel
and Kim Blundell

Music selected, arranged and edited by Anthony Marks
New compositions by Anthony Marks
Piano advisor: John York
Music setting: Andrew Jones
Managing designer: Russell Punter

About this book

You will already know some of these tunes, though others might be less familiar. Three of them were written specially for this book. If you have a computer, you can listen to all the tunes on the Usborne Quicklinks Website to hear how they go. Just go to **www.usborne-quicklinks.com** and enter the keywords "very easy piano tunes", then follow the simple instructions.

At the top of every piece there is a picture in a circle. Each of these has a sticker to match in the middle of the book. Use these to show that you have learned the piece. There are star stickers too, to use if you or your teacher think you play a piece very well.

Contents

Merrily we roll along

This tune is an old American song. It is also the same tune as the nursery rhyme "Mary had a little lamb". Nobody knows which came first.

The second part of this tune is a little bit harder than the first, as you have to play more notes in the left hand. You could start with the first half, and learn the second half later.

À la claire fontaine

This is a French-Canadian tune. Its title means "By the clear fountain". French people first went to live in Canada in the 17th century.

Get some other people to join in with this tune. They can play the music below on the violin, keyboard, guitar, chime bars or recorder. (You could copy this out to make it easier to read.)

For an easier part, someone could play the notes F and C in time with the left hand of the piano. Before you begin playing, count a few bars together so that everybody starts at the same time.

On the riverbank

This is an old tune from eastern Europe. Play it smoothly without gaps between the notes. Does it sound better fast or slow?

The grand old Duke of York

This tune was written in the 18th century. The Duke of York was the son of King George III of England. He fought wars in France and Holland.

Ask someone to add the rhythm on the right while you play this tune. They begin where you see the drummer in the music and play the pattern all the way through. They can clap, tap with a pencil on a table, or use a drum.

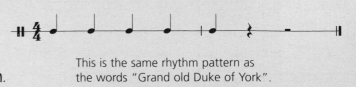

This is the same rhythm pattern as the words "Grand old Duke of York".

The knight's song

This is a very old French tune. There are lots of French songs about knights and castles that were written by wandering musicians called troubadours.

You could make this tune sound very old and mysterious. Ask someone to play it with you on the recorder, and get someone else to play a drum, beating the rhythm of the first bar all the way through the music.

Do you think it sounds better played quickly or slowly?

Sur le pont d'Avignon

This is a French tune. The title means "On the bridge at Avignon", though people used to dance on an island in the river under the bridge, not on top of it.

London Bridge is falling down

The Romans first built London Bridge, probably out of wood. It had to be rebuilt many times because the River Thames kept sweeping it away.

When you know both these tunes, play them one after the other. Do they sound right if you play them the same speed? Or does one work better a little faster than the other?

People used to dance to "Sur le pont d'Avignon" . . .

. . . but "London Bridge" is more like marching music.

Au clair de la lune

This French tune was written in the 17th century. Some people say it is by a famous composer named Jean-Baptiste Lully who worked at the court of the French king. The title means "In the moonlight".

Ask someone to add bells to this tune. Use chime bars, a glockenspiel or a bell sound on an electronic keyboard. You will need the notes C, D, E and F. Play each one for two beats, in the order shown below.

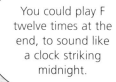

You could play F twelve times at the end, to sound like a clock striking midnight.

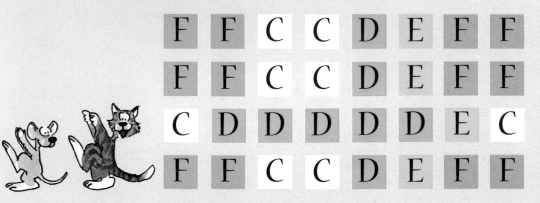

F	F	C	C	D	E	F	F
F	F	C	C	D	E	F	F
C	D	D	D	D	E	C	
F	F	C	C	D	E	F	F

Oh, dear, what can the matter be?

This Scottish song was written around 1770. It is also known as "Johnny's so long at the fair". Learn the first part before going on to the second half, which is a bit more difficult.

Temple bell

This tune was written specially for this book. Play it slowly, keeping in rhythm. See if you can make the last note sound like a bell.

Using the three patterns here, other people could add bell sounds while you play "Temple bell". This works well with chime bars, or a bell sound on an electronic keyboard.

1

2

3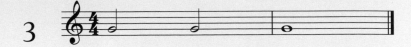

In time with the piano music, play pattern 1 three times, then pattern 2 three times, then pattern 1 twice. Pattern 3 will work all the way through, and goes with the other patterns as well.

Count a few bars before you begin so that everyone starts at the same time.

Play a C or a G to go with the last bar of the piano music.

Bobby Shafto

"Bobby Shafto" was first sung in the north of England in the 18th century. It is about a sailor who goes away to sea.

Sometimes tunes move by steps on the keyboard, from one key to the one next to it. Sometimes they move by jumps, and you have to leave out some keys. Which of these two tunes has more steps? Which has more jumps?

Streets of Laredo

This is an old cowboy tune. Laredo is a city in Texas, near the border between America and Mexico. Watch out for the F sharps.

On this page and the next three, there are hints about adding other instruments to make the tunes sound like cowboy music. Don't worry if you don't have all the instruments or enough players.

Violin or recorder: Play the right hand part, smoothly and gently. Cello: Play the left hand part, or just the first note of each bar, plucking the strings instead of bowing.

Billy boy

This tune is now more popular in the USA, but was probably first sung in Britain and taken to America in the 18th or 19th century. Look out for the B flats.

Guitar: the tunes on pages 14-17 all have guitar chords. Strum each chord once. Where there is no chord symbol, leave a gap. The chords you need for these tunes are shown in the window on the right.

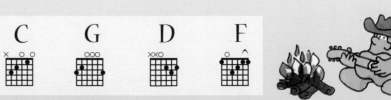

Home on the range

This American song was written in the 1870s by Brewster Higley and Daniel Kelley. It is now the state song of Kansas.

Long, long ago

Thomas Haynes Bayley, an English poet, wrote this in 1833. In 1843 it was published in America, where it was very popular for many years.

Electronic keyboard: you could add a rhythm accompaniment to the pieces on pages 14-17. Choose "4-beat" for the tunes in 4/4 and "waltz" or "country waltz" for the ones in 3/4.

Percussion: use cowbells, claves or temple blocks. Try a high sound on the first beat of each bar, then a lower sound for the rest.

See page 15 for more about the guitar chords above the music for these two tunes.

Where, oh where, has my little dog gone?

This tune was published in America in 1864 by the composer Septimus Winner. He based it on a German song about a man who loses his socks.

The notes at the beginning and end of the right hand part are imitations of a dog barking. You might be able to think of other ways to imitate this sound, either on a piano or another instrument.

Stone, sea, sky

This tune was written specially for this book. Don't rush the shorter notes, and watch out for accidentals. Does it sound better loud or quiet?

Silent night

"Silent night" was written in Oberndorf, Austria, by a teacher named Franz Gruber and a priest named Josef Mohr. It was first performed on Christmas Eve, 1818.

Some people say that the church organ was broken that night, so Gruber used a guitar. A guitarist could play the chords above the music while you play the tune. (Find out more about these chords on page 15.) Someone else could play the right hand part on the violin or recorder.

How far is it to Bethlehem?

Nobody knows who wrote this English Christmas carol, but it is hundreds of years old. Play it slowly and quietly.

The last four bars are a short ending section called a coda. (Coda is the Italian word for "tail".) It makes the tune sound finished. You could try writing a coda of your own. Experiment until you find an ending you like, then write it down.

Scarborough fair

This English tune was first sung in the middle ages. Once a year there was a huge market and fair in the seaside town of Scarborough.

Watch out for the tied notes. Make sure you hold them for their full length.

Does this tune sound best played quickly or slowly? Play it a few times in different ways and decide which you like best. (You can do this with any of the other tunes in this book too.)

Lavender's blue

This is a 17th-century English song. Lavender is a sweet-smelling plant. People believed it would help them sleep and give them pleasant dreams.

Don't rush the short notes!

Try playing the first bar of the right hand in lots of different ways.

First, try playing all three notes smoothly, joining them together as much as possible.

Then make the first two notes smooth, but make the third one shorter and a bit spiky.

Then try playing the first note smoothly but make the second and third spiky.

Which do you like best? Once you have decided, use that pattern to play every bar that has this rhythm.

23

Frère Jacques

The title of this old French song means "Brother James". It is about a monk. Your two hands play the same tune, but not at the same time. This is called a round.

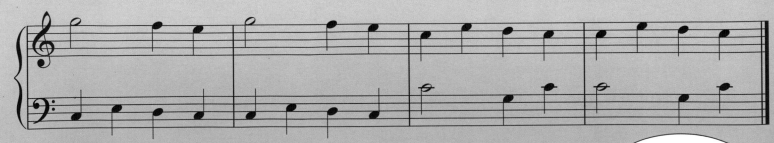

The first half of this tune is the original version of "Frère Jacques". The second half is a new tune that uses the same notes, but not in the same order. Can you work out what has been done to them?

Clue: Start at the end and play backwards!

Michael, row the boat ashore

This tune is a spiritual. Spirituals were first sung in America in the early 19th century. For the left hand part, think of a boat bobbing on water.

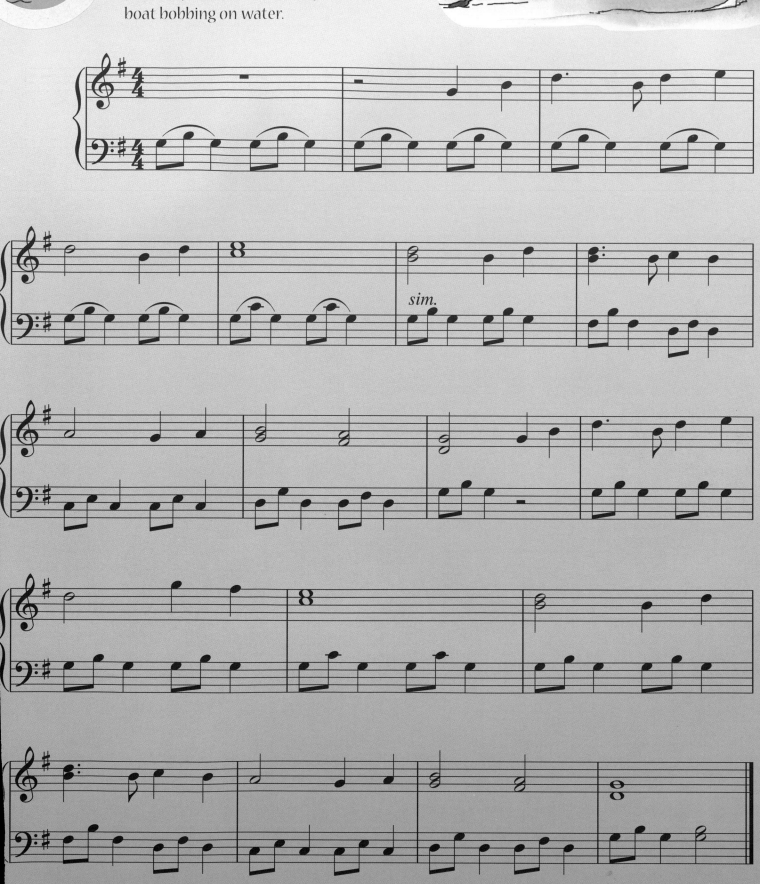

When the saints go marching in

This is another spiritual. Spirituals were first sung by African slaves in the southern USA. They are religious songs, and many are based on old African folk tunes.

Look out for the repeats!

Triumphantly!

Play this tune a few times, sometimes loudly, sometimes quietly. Which do you prefer? Try playing some parts loud, others quiet. Does it sound better if you get loud suddenly or gradually?

Island song

This tune was written specially for this book. Count the rests in the second half very carefully, as some of them come in unexpected places.

Smoothly

27

Turn the glasses over

This is a sailor's song called a sea shanty. "Shanty" comes from the French word "chanter", which means "to sing". You can find some of the words below.

Swaggering

I've been to Haarlem, I've been to Dover
I've travelled this wide world all over!
Over, over, three times over,
Drink what you've got to drink
and turn the glasses over!

Sailing east, sailing west
Sailing over the ocean,
Better watch out
when the boat begins to rock
Or you'll lose your girl in the ocean!

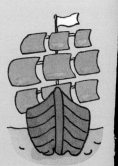

What shall we do with the drunken sailor?

Sailors sang shanties while they were doing hard work like pulling ropes. The rhythm of the music helped them keep time, which made the work easier.

Sailors used instruments they could carry easily, like fiddles, whistles and drums. You could ask someone to play these tunes with you on the violin or recorder, or beat a drum, or pencil on a table, to keep time.

Auld lang syne

This is a Scottish song first written down in the 18th century by the poet Robert Burns. People sing it on New Year's Eve. The title means "Old times".

The repeated notes in the left hand imitate the long sound made by bagpipes, called a drone. This tune is often played on the bagpipes in Scotland. To imitate this, ask someone to play the lowest left-hand notes on a cello, or use the bagpipe sound on a keyboard.

We wish you a merry Christmas

This English tune was written in England in the 19th century in the reign of Queen Victoria. This was also when Christmas cards were invented.

Notes for teachers

Very Easy Piano Tunes is an ideal first repertoire book. It can either be used along with a primer or - with a little explanation from a teacher - on its own. For more advanced pupils, it is an ideal sight-reading resource - it is designed for browsing and entertainment. As well as being fun, the stickers can be used as a progress record and to promote self-assessment.

The pieces at the beginning are progressive in difficulty. Pupils can play the first six pieces without changing the position of either hand. For the next six pieces, the left hand remains static while the range of the right is slowly enlarged. After this the order of difficulty is less strict, but new musical and technical concepts are introduced gradually. In particular the pieces are intended to encourage the development of a good sense of pulse and the independence of the hands.

Markings such as dynamics and fingerings are kept to a minimum. This is partly to respect the technical abilities of beginners, and partly to leave room for the teacher's own comments and preferences.

The three new compositions are positioned in the book to exploit the skills that have been learned on earlier pages. They also provide an introduction to techniques, sonorities and harmonies that young pupils may not otherwise encounter.

The extra activities are designed to expand pupils' musicianship, to encourage pianists to play with other people and to provide opportunities for transferring skills learned in the piano lesson into the classroom. They also explore some of the challenges pupils will meet both in the aural and musicianship sections of music exams, and in the requirements for music in the school curriculum.

You can listen to all the tunes in this book on the Usborne Quicklinks Website. Go to **www.usborne-quicklinks.com** and enter the keywords "very easy piano tunes", then follow the instructions.

First published in 2003 by Usborne Publishing Ltd, Usborne House, 83-85 Saffron Hill, London EC1N 8RT, England.
www.usborne.com